ROYAL FLEET AUXILIARY
IN FOCUS

Jon Wise

INTRODUCTION

At the end of the nineteenth century, the Royal Navy was a truly global force served by a complex logistical network including a large number of ships both Admiralty owned and under charter. Already, in 1864, an Order-in-Council had determined that all mercantile crewed "auxiliaries" should wear the Blue Ensign defaced by the Admiralty seal or badge.

The introduction of steam, and with it the requirement to move vast amounts of coal, had accelerated the need for rationalisation. This came about initially with an Admiralty circular letter in August 1905 directing that the title "Royal Fleet Auxiliary" be applied to Admiralty owned vessels manned by mercantile crews. This distinguished them from merchantmen on transport charter which were to be known as "Mercantile Fleet Auxiliaries" (MFA). However, the legal position of these newly titled vessels within the framework of the Merchant Shipping Acts initially proved irreconcilable and was only clarified once an Admiralty Order-in-Council had been issued in 1911. It was a further two years before the term Royal Fleet Auxiliary (RFA) appeared for the first time in the Navy List.

Initially there were only four Admiralty owned vessels which fitted this new title: the oil tank vessel PETROLEUM, the collier KHARKI, the distilling ship AQUARIUS and the hospital ship MAINE. In 1908, the then Director of Stores (DoS), Sir John Forsey, prompted the Admiralty to instigate what became the RFA's first construction programme, the five-strong 2000 ton Class. They were designated "Fleet Attendant Oilers" and could refuel more than one warship at a time while alongside.

By the summer of 1914 the strength of the RFA had only increased to seven vessels with a further three completing and four under construction. The sluggish growth rate can be attributed to several factors. Firstly, MFA colliers were employed to maintain suitable stockpiles at home and abroad. Secondly, although there was an increasing demand for oil by the fleet, it was only in 1912 that a report had recommended that it would be more economical in the long run to freight supplies using Admiralty owned tankers. By the outbreak of World War One there was just one ocean-going tanker on the stocks, the experimental 8000-ton RFA OLYMPIA (later SANTA MARGHERITA)

Finally, it was accepted practice that warships would continue to be coaled while in harbour. Coaling-at-Sea experiments, undertaken between 1902-1912, had shown the evolution to be impractical. Trial gear fitted in RFA PETROLEUM in 1906 resulted in the world's first oiling-at-sea experiments. A flexible bronze hose was passed to the battleship HMS VICTORIOUS, using a rig known as the "stirrup method". The experiments, later with HMS DOMINION, involved both the battleship leading PETROLEUM and vice versa.

Despite demonstrating the feasibility of the oiling-at-sea concept, pre-war it was considered both unnecessary and uneconomical to develop Replenishment at Sea (RAS) techniques further. This perception lasted and although experiments continued after 1918, the laborious and inefficient stirrup method was not entirely superseded by the "trough method" until the 1939-45 conflict.

If the Royal Navy entered World War One primarily as a coal-burning fleet it finished the war primarily as an oil-burning one. This revolution resulted in a rapid expansion in RFA flagged vessels, mainly in the 1916-18 period.

However, neither the infrastructure nor the expertise was in place in the twenties for the DoS to run over forty freighting tankers. During World War One many Admiralty owned oilers had been placed under commercial management. For example, it was perceived as diplomatically convenient for Messers Lane and MacAndrew (of the neutral United States) to be seen as managing the 5,000 ton Leaf Class which were tasked with freighting oil across the North Atlantic.

The practice was allowed to continue in the inter-war years. Despite the fact that the Admiralty had ordered the DoS to expedite the transfer from commercial management, the last four vessels only left British Tanker Company (BTC) control just prior to the outbreak of World War Two. A number were managed by the BTC and by the Anglo-Saxon Petroleum Company, while smaller vessels passed to Yard Craft manning. During this period the Treasury, rather than the Admiralty, earned valuable revenue when both RFA manned and commercially managed tankers were run on voyage charters for commercial companies.

Aside from the oil (and spirit) tankers and the hospital ship, the small number of other RFA vessels were principally stores carriers, some with an additional water distilling function. An exception was the fleet repair ship RFA RELIANCE. Crewed by the Merchant Navy, with a repair staff drawn from the three Royal Dockyards and a RN Engineer Captain, the ship was an interesting early example of mixed manning.

The impending war with Germany prompted naval rearmament but there was no corresponding RFA building programme, rather the prospect of the block obsolescence of its tanker fleet in the late thirties and early forties. However, due to the foresight of the DoS, Sir William Gick, the Admiralty subsequently acquired from BTC six 12,000 tons dwt. diesel tankers then under construction or projected. At the outbreak of war these vessels (the Dales), with two further additions to the class, were easily the most modern ships in a 61 strong tanker fleet of which nine were in reserve.

The early years of World War Two resulted in comparatively few additions to RFA numbers but the first steps were taken towards what would be a revolution in replenishment practices. Prior to 1937, RAS experiments had concentrated on the astern method of fuelling. That year a series of abeam refuelling trials was undertaken. A 3¹/₂ inch flexible bronze pipe was suspended by means of a light steel trough from the head of a derrick sited amidships in the tanker and passed in a catenary to the receiving warship. However, there were problems with this, not least of which was the suction effect caused by the interaction of the bow waves of two vessels steaming in close proximity - despite the restraining influence of double 8-inch manilla springs.

The capture of three German supply tankers in 1942 provided a much needed breakthrough. One discovery was the enemy's successful use of inflatable rubber hoses. Rubber hoses at once proved much lighter and more manageable to handle than bronze and this importantly resulted in shorter replenishment times. Other refinements which were to improve abeam refuelling practices included the fitting of substantial "goalpost" style gantries from which much longer derricks could be suspended. These derricks, coupled with an extensive system of blocks, allowed two or more troughs to be used, thus reducing the risk of broken pipes which had hampered earlier trials. The use of rubber hoses also proved particularly successful in astern refuelling which was still the favoured replenishment style.

The considerable logistical problems posed by the war in the Pacific in 1944-45 have been well documented. Not only had the British Pacific Fleet (BPF) been required to be fully self-supporting but RAS had to be conducted using tankers capable of sustaining 15-knots during replenishment serials. The 12-knot Dales were inadequate for this purpose and this led to the RFA acquiring what became the numerous Wave Class.

The war ended with the service apparently on the verge of fundamental changes in the ways in which it serviced the requirements of the Royal Navy. The ageing mainstays of the surviving inter-war tanker fleet, including the Leaf, War and 1000 ton Classes, were all destined to be scrapped.

However, the comparatively new Ranger Class built in the period 1940-41, the war construction 1,500 ton Class and slightly later Eddy Class, all classified as Fleet Attendant Tankers, appeared for a time to perpetuate the RFA's traditional role.

It was the arrival of the purpose-built Tide Class of Fast Fleet Tanker in the mid-1950's which heralded a true shift in focus. Several of the Wave Class were also fully modernized in order to boost the number capable of supporting sustained naval operations away from base. Furthermore, the lessons in self-sufficiency demanded of the BPF eventually led to the RFA acquiring eight Fort Class freighters. By the time these had joined the service a few years after the war they had been converted into specialist stores ships thus greatly expanding the profile of a hitherto minor portion of the RFA's operation. The "heavy jackstay" method of dry stores replenishment was developed and this, together with early vertical replenishment (VERTREP) trials using helicopters, signalled further significant advances.

A series of Defence Reviews in the period 1951-57 argued the case for the Royal Navy to plan for limited war and peacekeeping tasks in relatively distant areas of the globe, later clarified as being principally East of Suez. During the sixties, the RFA's part in supporting this strategy incorporated an extensive building programme. In 1960, a paper entitled "The Concept of Afloat Support" envisaged the RFA providing two Underway Replenishment Groups (URG) East of Suez each capable of sustaining a carrier group for prolonged periods with fuel, ammunition, naval and air stores. Three distinct types of auxiliary were defined, in turn specialising in front line, forward base and freighting support.

Apart from the Tides, existing tankers were considered inadequate for the front-line support task. This resulted in the building of the highly capable Improved Tide and Ol Classes which could operate in any climatic environment and whose design incorporated helicopter platforms, hangars and associated maintenance facilities. Around the same time a new Leaf Class was progressively introduced, with varying amounts of RAS capability, in order principally to undertake base support and freighting functions.

By the end of the decade two types of Fleet Replenishment Ship, the Resource and Ness Classes, had been constructed to replace the elderly Forts. The function of these five vessels, together with three other converted ships, was to provide the full range of dry stores for supporting a continuous thirty day task group operation. The ships boasted the latest in automated equipment for rapid cargo transfer. All the new-build were fitted with VERTREP facilities.

The abandonment of the CVA-01 carrier project in 1966, followed less than a year later by the announcement of a timetable for a phased withdrawal from East of Suez by 1975, was traumatic for the Navy but came too late to affect the RFA's building plans. The last part of the replacement programme, the Rover Class of small fleet tanker, was about to enter service. Moreover, the latter half of the decade brought unexpected diversification as firstly the new helicopter training ship ENGADINE joined the service in 1967 followed by the six Sir Lancelot Class Landing Ship Logistic (LSL) in 1970. Both acquisitions were the result of pragmatic decisions based on manpower shortages at the time but the success of the RFA in operating these vessels in the last quarter of the century ensured that their replacements, ARGUS and the Bay Class Alternative Landing Ship Logistic (ALSL), either have been or will be RFA manned.

Unsurprisingly, in recent years successive replacement programmes have mirrored the downsizing of the Royal Navy. Thus five 1980's Leaf Class Support / Freighting Tankers replaced a total of ten 1960's vintage Leaf and Dale Classes. At the end of the 1970's there were nine Fleet Replenishment Ships, at the time of writing there are just four.

However reductions have been in reverse proportion to capability. From the 1960's onwards, RFAs have been fitted with increasingly sophisticated communications, navigational equipment, NBCD facilities and passive self-defence in the form of IFF, ESM and rocket decoy launchers. Helicopters have added a further dimension as "force multipliers" enabling, for example, all four of the current Forts to carry sonobuoys and naval air weapons for their embarked ASW flights.

The status of RFAs as merchant ships traditionally allowed them to enter foreign ports without diplomatic clearance. In recent years, and particularly since 1982 when it was decided that auxiliaries should be fitted with rather than for defensive weapons, all RFAs have tended to require this clearance. This factor, together with the historical events of the last thirty years of the 20th Century, have served to blur many of the distinctions between the operational roles of the RN and RFA and these are chronicled elsewhere in this book.

A senior RFA officer once famously described the relationship between his service and the RN as "a shotgun marriage between the hunter and the provider". This is no longer the case. Mixed manning has become the accepted norm, especially since the introduction of helicopters on board auxiliaries in the early 1960's. Moreover, changes in the command structure over the last decade have led to further integration. In 1993 the RFA Flotilla became part of Fleet Command with the Commodore moving to Portsmouth. Plans announced in 2001 to bring the RN Fleet Headquarters to Whale Island, Portsmouth, also impact on the RFA. The service will be line-managed by the Deputy C-in-C Fleet at Portsmouth while the Commodore, assuming the somewhat cumbersome title of Chief of Staff (Sustainability), will be responsible not only for the RFA but also for Maritime Logistics, Land Logistics and the RN Supply Organisation.

The RFA continues to be the acknowledged world leader in the provision of its specialist and highly skilled type of support. The fact that it has prospered in its unique form and under its current mandate for nearly 100 years, in the face of periodic suggestions that its tasks should be undertaken by the Royal Navy, sub-divided among different organisations or even privatised, offers the finest tribute to the men and women who have contributed to its long and distinguished history.

I am indebted to the staff of the Public Relations Office COMRFA who permitted me access to their photographic archive. I am also grateful to Thomas A. Adams for his help particularly on matters related to the organisation of the service. However, my special thanks are reserved for First Officer James R. Smith RFA whose enthusiasm, eye for detail and encyclopaedic knowledge of this subject have proved indispensable in compiling this book.

Jon Wise
April 2002

RFA PETROLEUM

The purchase of an oil tank vessel in March 1905, which subsequently became RFA PETROLEUM, marked a significant milestone for the nascent service. Tasks pioneered by this vessel have become integral to the RFA's role ever since. It was intended that the 9,900 tons Swan Hunter ship, built in 1903, should follow the Atlantic Fleet on cruises so that she could be towed behind a battleship and oil could be pumped via a flexible hose in "any ordinary weather at sea". In harbour PETROLEUM would refuel HM ships alongside in the "fleet attendant" role. From 1908-1914 she evaluated the cost-effectiveness of government, rather than commercial, vessels undertaking the oil freighting duties. PETROLEUM was fleet attendant tanker at Scapa Flow throughout World War I, her lengthy RFA career ending in 1935.

(RFA Archive)

RFA KHARKI

RFA KHARKI photographed underway off Hong Kong Island in the early 1920's while serving on the China Station. This small, coal-burning ship, with a 680 tons oil cargo capacity, was built in 1899 by Irvine Shipbuilding and Engineering and purchased as a yard collier by the Admiralty the following year. KHARKI was converted to a tanker in 1906/7 and was then based at Portland until 1920. Her subsequent eleven year career in the Far East was interrupted in 1924 when the ship was severely damaged by a typhoon. Following her sale to a Chinese firm in 1931, KHARKI was converted back to a dry-cargo carrier. (RFA Archive)

RFA MERCEDES

Coaling-at-sea trials had been conducted in the first few years of the century using chartered mercantile colliers and in 1908 the Admiralty purchased what became RFA MERCEDES in order further to evaluate an evolution so dependent on reliable equipment and favourable sea conditions. MERCEDES was considered "state of the art" with four large holds served by spacious hatches and extra long derricks. Fitted with a modified Metcalfe Rig for coaling experiments in 1910, she carried out trials at sea with HMS DOMINION two years later. These inconclusive experiments marked the end of the Admiralty's interests in this concept. Otherwise, MERCEDES, photographed here after her RFA career had ended, was mainly employed in the freighting role between home ports. She was sold in 1920.

(RFA Archive)

RFA BURMA

The origins of the five, broadly similar First 2,000 ton Class can be traced to 1908 when the RN's increasing demand of oil required appropriate means of transportation. These Admiralty designed ships constituted the first RFA oiler construction programme. BURMA, the first of class, was launched in March 1911 as a fleet attendant oiler with an alongside capability utilising four replenishment points. Her 2,000 tons oil capacity was distributed among twelve tanks the system being managed by a pumproom operator who controlled the ingress and discharge of the cargo. In November 1911, BURMA undertook oiling-at-sea trials with HMS AGAMEMNON. Arguably the most successful of this experimental class, the ship's fifteen year spell on active service ended in 1926. She was scrapped nine years later.

(RFA Archive)

RFA CAROL

The second pre-WWI oiler construction programme produced the so-called First 1,000 ton Class. The four ships, including CAROL here, were shallow-draught vessels more akin to powered barges and intended for harbour use. All were built in UK Royal Dockyards; the 1,935 tons CAROL was completed at Devonport in 1914. She and her sister FEROL were engined with Bolinder diesel motors. These early diesels proved troublesome with CAROL's maiden voyage to Liverpool taking three months, including breakdowns. She was used in the harbour attendant role until entering the reserve in 1925. She was sold for scrap a decade later. The far more numerous war-construction Second 1,000 ton Class enjoyed long and successful service lives in marked contrast to this quartet.   (RFA Archive)

RFA INDUSTRY (1901)

RFA INDUSTRY, the service's first store carrier, was not RFA manned until 1914 having been operated prior to that by local dockyard employees under the Yard Craft scheme. The small 800 grt ship was built by William Beardmore at Glasgow and fitted with a triple expansion engine driving a single screw. INDUSTRY was constructed on traditional freighter lines with midships engines and bridge together with holds fore and aft, a design which has been imitated by successive RFA dry stores ships. She was torpedoed while under escort in October 1918 but managed to reach port. The ship was sold the following year. (RFA Archive)

RFA RUTHENIA

The former RUTHENIA lying in the Johore Strait near HM Dockyard, Singapore just after the war. This 7,239 grt former passenger/cargo ship, built in 1900, was purchased by the Admiralty in 1914 and promptly used as a dummy battleship. Although originally earmarked as a storeship she was taken in hand the following year for conversion to a tanker, with cylindrical tanks in her cargo holds. Re-named RFA RUTHENIA in 1916 she served at Scapa Flow for two years and post-war on the China Station. By 1927 worn out boilers brought relegation to oil fuel jetty and pumping station at Singapore. Although scuttled in the face of the Japanese advance she was later raised and used as the troopship CHORAN MARU. Recovered in 1945, she was finally sold for scrap the following year. (RFA Archive)

RFA BACCHUS (1915)

RFA BACCHUS entering Valletta Harbour, Malta with naval stores, service passengers and additional deck cargo including a whaler and steam pinnace. She was employed on a regular Chatham/Gibraltar/Malta run in the inter-war years making her a popular appointment with RFA officers. BACCHUS was built by William Hamilton of Port Glasgow in 1915 and, from the outset, was operated by the Director of Stores as a naval ship with RFA manning. The 3,500 tons ship was a coal burner with a 2,000 tons cargo capacity. Although BACCHUS was originally classed as a repair ship, she was principally used as a stores carrier and distilling ship. She was replaced by BACCHUS II in 1936.

(RFA Archive)

RFA SANTA MARGHERITA

The 7,513 tons SANTA MARGHERITA (ex-OLYMPIA) was an RFA for just three years between 1916-19. However, her Admiralty design incorporated a number of advanced features. Built by Vickers at Barrow, the ship was engined with two eight cylinder diesel engines which proved embarrassingly unreliable very early in her career. This large ocean-going ship, with her classic tanker profile, had a 19,000 mile radius at 11 knots on her twin screws and carried a sizeable cargo of 8,200 tons of oil. She was equipped with electric auxiliaries, electric tank ventilation fans and two electric cargo pumps with a 150 tons per hour capability. SANTA MARGHERI-TA was fitted with bronze hoses and stirrups for replenishing at sea; her fuel lines are visible on the upper working deck. The ship's lengthy post-RFA career ended in 1950.

(James R. Smith Collection)

RFA TURMOIL

Whereas the second and third vessels of the experimental First 2,000 ton Class, MIXOL and THERMOL, suffered stability problems, the next pair, TREFOIL and TURMOIL (photographed here) proved mechanically unsatisfactory. These two ships, although similar in appearance and cargo capacity to BURMA, had a larger gross tonnage. In common with four other pre-WW1 auxiliaries, TURMOIL was built in a Royal Dockyard, at Pembroke Dock, and was fitted with steam triple expansion reciprocating engines by Ross and Duncan of Glasgow. Admiralty Instructions of the day required watertube boilers to be cleaned every three weeks which naturally curtailed the operational availability of the ship. TURMOIL was relegated to the reserve as early as 1923 and sold for scrap in 1935.

(RFA Archive)

RFA BIRCHOL

The tanker BIRCHOL was one of the eighteen strong, war construction, Second 1,000 ton Class which were all built in the period 1916-18. BIRCHOL had a 1,000 tons cargo capacity, her single screw triple expansion engine driving the ship at a speed of 9.5 knots. The design, with bridge and charthouse perched on top of the forecastle, was criticised at the time but proved efficient in service. In order to improve sea-keeping qualities and reduce fire risk, the ships were cut away over the tank tops leaving the expansion trunk plating as the only upper deck between forecastle and poop. She was lost in November 1939, having been stranded in the Hebrides.

(RFA Archive)

RFA ELDEROL
The durability of the WW1 vintage oilers of the Second 1,000 ton Class was exemplified by ELDEROL which was not sold for scrap until 1959 following a forty two year career. In common with most vessels of her type, she served in the fleet attendant role in various UK dockyards providing alongside replenishment for warships. During the inter-war period several of these tankers were operated by dockyard employees under the Yard Craft Agreement. They reverted to RFA manning and management in 1939. ELDEROL's midships tank section is clearly visible in this photograph of her underway.

(RFA Archive)

RFA DELPHINULA

The tanker DELPHINULA's nineteen year service in the RFA began in 1917 when she was purchased from a Japanese firm by the Anglo-Saxon Petroleum Company on behalf of the Admiralty. This photograph of her at sea as BUYO MARU was taken during the previous ownership when she carried oil from California to Japan. Good endurance and a sizeable 7,000 tons deadweight cargo capacity made DELPHINULA suitable for the transatlantic Chatham/Bermuda/Trinidad run freighting naval stores outbound and returning with oil. She was built by Armstrong Whitworth in 1908; her North Eastern Marine Engineering single screw triple expansion engine drove the ship at 10 knots. DELPHINULA's disproportionately tall funnels contribute to her singularly ungainly appearance.   (RFA Archive)

RFA SLAVOL

The ten Second 2,000 ton Class vessels (in common with the scaled-up 5,000 ton Leaf Class) were fitted with amidships engines giving them a radically different profile from earlier war-construction RFA tankers. Most, including SLAVOL here, were handsome looking ships with raked funnels and masts. Following their completion in 1917-18, war losses apart, the class provided sterling service across five decades. They had a cargo capacity of 2,150 tons of oil and stowage for 5,000 gallons of lubricating oil. Some had exceeded fifteen knots on trials but heavy fuel consumption tended to limit speeds to 11-12 knots, running on two boilers. SLAVOL was sunk by U-205 in the Mediterranean in March 1942.

(RFA Archive)

RFA FRANCOL

RFA FRANCOL at anchor, probably in the early twenties, when it was customary for a while for China Station ships to adopt a light grey/dark grey colour scheme. FRANCOL, together with MONTENOL and SERBOL, with their single upright mast and funnel, assumed less aesthetically pleasing profiles than the remainder of the Second 2,000 ton Class when their mainmasts were removed. Built by Earle's Shipbuilding and Engineering of Hull, FRANCOL spent her RFA career mostly based at Hong Kong or Wei-Hai-Wei. In addition to station oiler duties she was used for target towing and some RAS trials. The tanker was caught by the Japanese fleet and sunk south of Java a matter of days after the crucial allied defeat at the Battle of the Java Sea. (RFA Archive)

RFA PETROBUS

The three Pet Class Spirit Carriers, the 1,024 tons PETROBUS, PETRELLA and PETRONEL were all built by Dunlop, Bremner and Co. Ltd. at Port Glasgow in 1918 and acquired by the Admiralty the same year. They were powered by steam single screw triple expansion machinery and carried a cargo of 300 tons. PETRONEL was later used as a water boat, accompanying the Atlantic Fleet on cruises. The ships of this class spent most of their service lives plying between UK bases with occasional spells on charter. Succeeded by the Sprite Class, PETRONEL and PETRELLA were sold in 1945 and 1946 respectively. PETROBUS was not disposed of until 1959 when she was sold to the British Iron and Steel Corporation for scrap. (RFA Archive)

RFA PLUMLEAF (1917)

This photograph of PLUMLEAF leaving Malta shows the fine lines of the 5,000 ton Fast Leaf Class tankers with their raked masts and broad funnel. During WW1 the Leaf Class were employed as escorts on the North Atlantic convoy run at the same time transporting up to 5,400 tons of their own cargo. They were fitted with four powerful and advanced cargo pumps. It was intended that they should maintain 14 knots at sea on their twin screw triple expansion machinery but this was impracticable due to high fuel consumption and the number of hands required to service the six boilers which functioned in two, entirely separate, boiler rooms. PLUMLEAF was declared a constructive total loss at Malta in 1942.

(RFA Archive)

RFA PEARLEAF (1917)

RFA PEARLEAF was built by William Gray at West Hartlepool and like her sisters was launched in 1917. All but one of the six Leaf Class were in reserve at Rosyth between 1922-26 before being placed on charter to the Anglo-Saxon Petroleum Company for periods of up to six years. PEARLEAF undertook naval freighting duties from 1930-34 and then, in company with APPLELEAF, departed for the Far East to relieve BELGOL and FORTOL at Hong Kong. In the inter-war years some RFAs adopted station colours when on foreign deployment, at the discretion of the local Commander-in-Chief. Here, PEARLEAF sports the white hull and light grey upperworks of the China Station. She remained in eastern waters for most of the war before disposal and scrapping in 1946.   (RFA Archive)

RFA BRAMBLELEAF (1917)
RFA BRAMBLELEAF dressed overall at Alexandria in October 1930 in honour of the Coronation of the King of Egypt. BRAMBLELEAF had been in reserve at Gibraltar between 1922-25 after which she joined the Mediterranean Fleet where she remained for the rest of her career. She was torpedoed off Mersa Alun, between Tobruk and Alexandria, in June 1942. Thirteen crew members were killed and the ship took on a 28 degree list. However, despite repeated air attacks, a naval salvage party carried out temporary repairs and she was towed to Alexandria. She saw further service as a fuelling hulk using her forward tanks only. BRAMBLELEAF was sold for scrap in 1947.

(RFA Archive)

RFA WAR BAHADUR

The first group of six War Class tankers, all built in the period 1918-19, were modified A and B Class WW1 Standard dry cargo ships. These six vessels were each fitted with five tanks providing a capacity of about 7,400 tons of oil. Judging by the overall grey paint scheme and the neglected appearance, this photograph of WAR BAHADUR was probably taken during WW2 at Devonport where she served as a fuel hulk. In January 1939 the ship had been struck by a freak wave off south west Ireland which swept away her bridge and boats. She had to be escorted home and did not put to sea again. Note the derricks fore and aft which served WAR BAHADUR's two dry cargo holds used for the transportation of naval stores.

(James R. Smith Collection)

RFA WAR AFRIDI

RFA WAR AFRIDI underway in 1931 while under the management of C.T. Bowring and Co. Ltd. The second group of eight War Class freighting tankers, which included WAR AFRIDI, were fitted with seven as opposed to five cargo tanks. Additionally, they were internally strengthened with extra bulkheads in an effort to reduce rivet leakage, a problem which beset the first group. Unfortunately, this modification did not prove successful. These vessels were considered good seaboats however, even in heavy seas. WAR AFRIDI was built by R.Duncan and Co. Ltd. of Port Glasgow in 1920 and spent the last years of her service life as a fuel hulk in Hong Kong. She was scrapped in 1950.

(Royal Naval Museum)

RFA WAR PINDARI

The seven-tank, 5,548 tons grt. WAR PINDARI was built by Lithgows Ltd. at Port Glasgow and engined with triple expansion machinery which provided a loaded speed of about 10 knots. Following WW1, various committees reviewed the self-protection measures which should be applied to RFA tankers. The agreed War Class fit included 1 x 4-inch (on some ships), 1 x 12pdr guns and paravane equipment. At the outbreak of World War II fourteen of the class were in service with four becoming war losses. WAR PINDARI herself was sold to an Italian company in 1952.

(RFA Archive)

RFA MAINE (1902)

RFA MAINE entering Portsmouth Harbour probably in 1935 when she was present for the Spithead Jubilee Review in honour of King George V. Geneva Convention rules were relaxed on this occasion to allow the removal of her hospital ship markings in order to act as a Government Guest Ship. The coal-burning, former P.S.N. liner had been purchased in 1920. She spent the majority of her long RFA career serving the Mediterranean Fleet, including spells as floating hospital for the Marsamuscetto based submarine and destroyer flotillas. The ship was damaged during an air-raid in 1941 at Alexandria and later, in 1946, ran aground while trying to reach the RN ships mined in the Corfu Channel. She was sold and broken up in 1947.   (Royal Naval Museum)

RFA NUCULA
NUCULA was briefly in RFA service between 1922-24. The 4,614 tons grt. tanker was built by Armstrong, Whitworth and Co. Ltd. in 1906 and was powered bysingle screw triple expansion machinery by the Wallsend Slipway Company. Prior to becoming NUCULA in 1917 she had carried the names HERMIONE and SOYO MARU. The Admiralty purchased the vessel in 1922 and she joined the China Station. In September of the following year, while at Wei-Hai-Wei, she was ordered to Nagasaki, Japan to act as Base Oiler during the Yokohama Earthquake Relief operations. She transferred to the Royal New Zealand Navy in 1924 to undertake the role of Fleet Attendant Oiler. This photograph shows NUCULA at anchor during her time under Anglo Saxon Petroleum Company ownership.

(A.Duncan)

RFA OLYNTHUS

BRITISH STAR (later RFA OLYNTHUS) is seen here with black hull and white upperworks, colours of the British Tanker Company (BTC). The six broadly similar 10,000 ton Class, which shared the "Ol" prefix in their names, had single screw steam triple expansion machinery producing a service speed of around ten knots. Three of the class, OLCADES, OLIGARCH and OLYNTHUS herself, were both BTC managed and manned until the mid-1930's when they came under the control of the Director of Stores. In December 1939, having refuelled Force G (AJAX, ACHILLES and EXETER) in difficult weather and about to witness the Battle of the River Plate, OLYN-THUS received the somewhat laconic signal, "If GRAF SPEE comes your way, let her through".   (RFA Archive)

RFA OLIGARCH

The 6,897 tons grt. RFA OLIGARCH (ex. BRITISH LANTERN) leaving South Shields in May 1943. Plans to disguise and defensively arm RFAs had been formulated and trialed in the immediate pre-war years. Disguises are evident here in the neutral paintwork and large dummy funnel aft of the midships superstructure. OLIGARCH's actual funnel has been reduced in size and is screened in order to present a conventional cargo ship profile to a potential enemy. Some of her armament is also visible including at least one 4-inch gun. The tanker, used for Russian Convoy work, was torpedoed in the Eastern Mediterranean in July 1943. OLIGARCH was towed to Alexandria where she continued to serve as a fuel hulk before being scuttled in the Red Sea in 1946. (RFA Archive)

RFA PERTHSHIRE

Built as a cargo and emigrant ship in 1893, RFA PERTHSHIRE enjoyed a long and chequered career under the red, white and blue ensigns. In 1899 she "disappeared" for 46 days in the Tasman Sea following the loss of her single propeller; a serious matter in pre-wireless days. In 1914 she was requisitioned by the Navy and converted into a dummy battleship in the guise of HMS VANGUARD. Later roles included coaling officer's ship, mobile hulk and naval stores carrier. In 1924-5 PERTHSHIRE was reconditioned and fitted out as a dedicated supply ship for refrigerated and general stores. This marked a further development for the RFA as PERTHSHIRE was the first large storeship to serve under the blue ensign. She worked with the Mediterranean Fleet in this role until replaced by RFA RELIANT in 1934.

(RFA Archive)

RFA RELIANT (1922)

RFA RELIANT photographed at Malta in the 1930's with a familiar cluster of dghaisas alongside. Purchased from the Furness Line in 1933 she replaced PERTHSHIRE as Mediterranean Fleet naval and victualling stores ship having the advantage of considerable refrigerated storage space. As supply depot ship for submarines and destroyers in Marsamuscetto, she survived the aerial assault on Malta before moving on to the Far East. She was sold in 1948. RELIANT was the third choice of name for the ship, PERTHSHIRE and RELIANCE already being in commercial use.

(RFA Archive)

RFA BACCHUS (1936)

The second stores ship to carry this name, BACCHUS replaced her namesake in 1936. Photographed in 1953, towards the end of her career, her rather dated lines derive from the fact that the design was closely based on her 1915 vintage predecessor. In common with the previous BACCHUS, this ship was subsequently fitted with a distilling plant in 1939. Converted into a Naval Stores Issuing Ship (NSIS) in 1942 she served first on the East Indies Station then in the Persian Gulf and later with the Pacific Fleet Train. Post-war she reverted to running stores from the UK to the Mediterranean and Far East until sold in 1962. She was scrapped in 1964.

(MoD/Crown Copyright)

RFA ARNDALE
Concern over the age of the existing tanker fleet in 1937 led to an initial purchase of six tankers, while under construction, from the British Tanker Company (BTC). The resulting Dale Class had a deadweight of 12,000 tons which was considerably greater than the preceding "War" and "Ol" Classes. Shown here undergoing trials in 1952, ARNDALE was fitted with a four cylinder Doxford engine in common with the other "A" Dales which provided a service speed of 12 knots. This was considered inadequate for fleet work when ARNDALE joined the British Pacific Fleet (BPF) at the end of the war. Nevertheless she took part in operations off Okinawa. The ship was laid up in Rosyth in 1959 and scrapped a year later in Belgium.

(RFA Archive)

RFA BISHOPDALE

Another member of the first group of Dales, BISHOPDALE is shown here running light in this 1954 photograph. During the early part of the war the tanker supported RN warships hunting blockade runners in the South Atlantic and South West Pacific. By 1945, BISH-OPDALE was with the BPF where she suffered considerable damage on 14 December 1944 from a Kamikaze bomber attack. Note she has retained her A.A. gun "bandstand" forward and gun positions on the bridge superstructure and abreast the funnel, a legacy of the war years. Laid up in 1959 she became a storage hulk at Devonport in 1966 before being scrapped in 1970 in Spain.

(MoD/Crown Copyright)

RFA CAIRNDALE

RFA CAIRNDALE was one of a pair of tankers purchased from the Anglo Saxon Petroleum Company in 1939 in order to compare the design with the "A" and "B" Dales. Similar in dimensions and capacity to the BTC ships the "C's" could be distinguished by the enlarged amidships superstructure and funnel stepped further aft. In common with the "B" Dales, CAIRNDALE was engined with an eight-cylinder Burmeister and Wain diesel providing a service speed of 11.5 knots. During the war she was initially a harbour oiler at Freetown before joining Force H at Gibraltar. On 30 May 1941, while operating west of Gibraltar, she was hit by two torpedoes from an Italian submarine, sinking in four minutes with the loss of four lives. CAIRNDALE was one of five Dales lost during the war.   (RFA Archive)

RFA ROBERT DUNDAS

Both ROBERT DUNDAS and her sister ROBERT MIDDLETON entered service in 1938 and were manned by local UK Dockyard employees under the Yard Craft Agreement before transferring to RFA manning in July 1940. Classed as a coastal stores carrier, ROBERT DUNDAS displayed modern, clean lines in comparison with BACCHUS completed just two years previously. The accommodation and machinery block sited aft allowed ample space for the two adjacent holds. No. 2 hatch, measuring 72 by 34 feet, was large enough to stow most types of naval stores then in service, including a landing craft. She took part in the Normandy landings in 1944. The ship was laid up at Chatham in December 1971 and scrapped eighteen months later.   (Fotoflite)

RFA ROBERT MIDDLETON

ROBERT MIDDLETON displaying the standard post-war RFA colour scheme of light grey overall with black boot-topping and broad black funnel band. Unusually for this period she lacked her pennant number A241. ROBERT MIDDLETON was fitted with an Atlas Polar six-cylinder diesel with single screw which gave her a maximum speed of 12 knots. The "Bobbys" had a loaded draught of 13.5 feet and were mainly employed in UK coastal waters although they did venture as far as Malta. In this photograph her usual load is augmented with an interesting deck cargo. Note the navigational radar on the mainmast and the additional mast stepped aft which distinguished ROBERT MIDDLETON from her sistership. Laid up in Rosyth in March 1975, the ship was sold commercially later that year.

(Fotoflite)

RFA BLACK RANGER

The six strong Ranger Class ships were built during 1940-41 as replacements for the 2000 ton Class. As such these were the first Admiralty designed tankers since the Leaf Class nearly a quarter of a century earlier. They carried a mixed cargo of 2,600 tons fuel oil, 550 tons diesel and 90 tons of petrol. The three "B" Rangers were engined with a six cylinder Harland-Burmeister and Wain diesel, the same size as the much larger Dale Class, making them exceptionally manoeuvrable. This 1961 photograph shows BLACK RANGER as FOST station tanker. The wheelhouse and funnel off-set to port and foremast on the starboard bow were wartime attempts to present a confusing silhouette to a potential enemy. She was sold overseas in 1973.

(MoD/Crown Copyright)

RFA GREEN RANGER

RFA GREEN RANGER, pictured here, together with GRAY RANGER and GOLD RANGER, were built by Caledon at Dundee whereas the "B" Rangers were Harland and Wolff ships. GREEN RANGER was further distinguished by being the first auxiliary to be used as a large spirit carrier although during the latter stages of the war in the Pacific she was converted into a water carrier. Note the prominent extension bridge for carrying hoses to the stern. The large forecastle was specially designed to accommodate a 9 ton RAF refuelling barge for flying boats although this facility was never used. GREEN RANGER was blown ashore on the Hartland Cliffs at Long Peak in November 1962 while being towed to refit and became a total loss.

(Fotoflite)

RFA DERWENTDALE (1941)

RFA DERWENTDALE belonged to the third group of Dale Class tankers, the "D" and "E" group, all of which were requisitioned by the Admiralty as part of the War Construction Programme. Built as a tanker, DERWENTDALE arrived at Liverpool in January 1943 to be converted to a Landing Ship Gantry (LSG), enabling her to carry up to 15 LCMs. Space was provided for the greatly increased complement in the forehold, in Nos. 8 and 9 tanks and on the bridge and stern superstructures. Post-war, DERWENTDALE, like her two LSG sisterships, had her gantry gear removed. However, as a freighting tanker on the Trinidad/U.K. run she utilised her existing passenger berths in the deckhouses aft which can be seen in this 1953 photograph. She was laid up at Rosyth in May 1959 and sold the same year.

(MoD/Crown Copyright)

RFA AIRSPRITE

RFA AIRSPRITE, together with her sistership NASPRITE, were Admiralty designed high-octane carriers intended mainly for coastal work. Built by Blythswood Shipbuilding Company, Glasgow AIRSPRITE entered service in 1943. She and her sister superseded the ageing Pet Class. Equipped with a three-cylinder triple expansion steam engine and single screw, AIRSPRITE had a service speed of eleven knots. The two ships spent the majority of their careers in home waters and in the Mediterranean. NASPRITE was sold for scrap in 1964 having been laid up for ten years. AIRSPRITE was placed in reserve at Devonport in 1963 and was sold to Belgian breakers less than two years later.

(RFA Archive)

RFA SALVAGE DUKE

The King Salvor Class RFA SALVAGE DUKE entering Portsmouth Harbour. One of twelve ocean salvage vessels of the class to be RFA manned (the thirteenth became the long-serving HMS RECLAIM), the 1,125 tons grt. SALVAGE DUKE was completed in November 1943 having been built by William Simons and Company in Renfrew. Several of this war construction class found their way into commercial charter post-war having seen limited service under the blue ensign. SALVAGE DUKE was chartered by the Turkish Navy in 1948 and in 1959 was gutted by fire while salvaging the tanker ISKENDERUN with the tragic loss of eleven of her crew.

(James R. Smith Collection)

RFA KINTERBURY

The naval armament carrier KINTERBURY was built by Philip and Son Ltd. of Dartmouth in 1943 as a replacement for NAV UPNOR. She was engined by Lobnitz and Company with coal-fired, triple expansion machinery which provided a speed of 11.5 knots and a range of 2,600 miles. It is interesting to note that, even in the 1940's, it was still a design requirement that KINTERBURY, and her sistership THROSK, should be capable of carrying the largest guns in the navy. In 1959, the two ships had their holds modified for the stowage of Sea Slug SAMs and were fitted with extra long (54 foot) derricks with 3 tons capacity for handling the missiles. This enabled them to serve as tenders for the guided weapons trials ship HMS GIRDLE NESS.

(Dave Scoble Collection)

RFA EMPIRE SALVAGE
The capture of the tanker LOTHRINGEN by the cruiser DUNEDIN in June 1941 subsequently proved a significant event in the long-term development of the RFA's abeam refuelling methods. Built by the Rotterdam Dry Dock Company as PAPENDRECHT, the 10,476 tons grt. vessel was requisitioned by the Germans in November 1940 and refitted to serve as one of BISMARCK's supply ships. Re-named RFA EMPIRE SALVAGE she was further modified for RFA work but more importantly, along with the other captured tankers NORDMARK (later HMS BULAWAYO) and GEDANIA provided vital information about German advances in RAS techniques using rubber hoses. RFA EMPIRE SALVAGE was returned to her owners in 1946 reverting to the name she carries in this photograph.

(James R. Smith Collection)

RFA WAVE KING

RFA WAVE KING was the first of the twenty strong class to be acquired by the Admiralty in 1944. Four completed in time to join the BPF where their speed, which varied from ship to ship, gave them up to a three knot advantage over the Dale Class. Originally planned to be diesel driven, the Waves were fitted with steam turbines and water tube boilers. These proved unreliable and expensive on fuel, initially consuming about fifty tons per day although the heavy fuel bills and repair costs were offset by lucrative charter work following the Korean War. The tanker's five roller fairlead for astern refuelling can be seen in this 1953 photograph which illustrates the original appearance of these tankers.

(MoD/Crown Copyright)

RFA WAVE PREMIER

RFA WAVE PREMIER displays the intermediate modification afforded many of this class with "goal-post" gantries fitted fore and aft of the bridge superstructure. The longer derricks, formerly used for anti-submarine net defence by merchant ships, were precursors of the purpose-built equipment fitted on the Tide and Ol Classes. These enabled the fuel hoses to be carried in more troughs, in turn allowing the ships to steam further apart during RAS serials. Nevertheless, the turbulence caused by this evolution was still considerable as illustrated in this photograph. WAVE PREMIER, together with LAIRD and RULER, kept this rig for most of their careers. Note that the ship has retained her forward gun platform, part of a 1950 directive. She also, unusually for the class, sports a funnel cap.

(MoD/Crown Copyright)

WAVE PREMIER

RFA WAVE KNIGHT (1945)

Eight of the Wave Class, including WAVE KNIGHT, were fully modified which brought them to a satisfactory standard for modern fleet work. These tankers were fitted with extra turbo cargo pumps and four seventy-foot derricks, all concentrated in the after-well. Other alterations included enlarged accommodation spaces on the bridge superstructure and a raised funnel. WAVE KNIGHT distinguished herself in 1962 by undertaking a marathon eighteen hour pump-over with RFA ORANGELEAF during a violent storm in the North Atlantic. Station keeping proved extremely difficult as winds reached Force 6/7 forcing the two tankers to close to within 50 feet of one another on occasions.

(MoD/Crown Copyright)

RFA SPABURN

The fourth in a class of six war construction 500 ton water tankers, SPABURN was built by Philip and Son Ltd. of Dartmouth. Part of the 1944 Estimates, she entered service in January 1946. In common with other vessels ordered in the latter stages of the war, SPABURN and her sisters were somewhat surplus to requirements and there were proposals for the laying up of at least some of the class. Consideration was also given to converting these ships to oil-burners in order to increase range and general usefulness if, as expected, their theatres of operation were to include the Mediterranean and the Far East. In the event this did not occur. The Spa Class later came under Port Auxiliary Service management.

(Dave Scoble Collection)

RFA ROWANOL
Variously known as the "1,500 ton Class" and the "Later Ol Class", ROWANOL and her three sisterships effectively replaced the WW1 vintage Second 1,000 ton Class of fleet attendant tankers when they entered service in 1946. They were all built by Lobnitz and Co. Ltd. and fitted with a single screw triple expansion engine. ROWANOL, whose previous names were EBONOL and CEDAROL, was based at Malta during the early part of her career where this photograph was taken. She was sold for scrap in 1971. (RFA Archive)

RFA OLNA (1945)

RFA OLNA, together with the eight fully modified Waves, provided the blueprint for the successful Tide and Ol class designs. Purchased while building from Shell and initially RN manned, OLNA transferred to the RFA in 1946 having been the most advanced of the BPF tankers during the last months of the war. Intended to run at speeds of up to 18 knots on her British Thomson-Houston turbo electric engines, in practice OLNA attained 15-16 knots. Used widely for replenishment trials post-war her appearance often altered. This 1953 photograph shows her with an "intermediate rig". She was present at the Coronation Fleet Review in June of that year, supported the Royal Navy during the First Cod War and was retired from service in 1966.   (MoD/Crown Copyright)

RFA MAINE (1943)

The hospital ship MAINE entering Grand Harbour, Malta in 1949. The 7,515 tons grt. former passenger /cargo ship was completed as the LEONARDO DA VINCI in Genoa in 1925. She was captured by the British off Somaliland in 1941 but her engines were later sabotaged causing serious turbine trouble. She eventually reached the USA via Bombay where repairs and conversion to a hospital ship were undertaken. She was transferred to RFA manning and management in January 1948 and named MAINE. By this time she was serving as RN Base Hospital Ship in Hong Kong with accommodation for 420 patients. MAINE supported the armed forces during the Korean War but in 1954 her hull and machinery were judged to be in a poor material condition and she was scrapped.

(RFA Archive)

RFA FORT DUNVEGAN

The war in the Pacific and the development of the Fleet Train concept underlined the need for stores carriers together with specialist armament (ASIS), naval (NSIS) and victualling (VSIS) issuing ships. Several of the Canadian Victory type, including FORT DUNVEGAN which completed as a refrigerated VSIS, served with the BPF before transferring to the RFA post-war. The five stores carriers, including FORT DUNVEGAN, together with the three dedicated armament ships, comprised the first homogenous class of ships of their type to serve in the RFA. The Forts were handicapped by their slow speed, attaining just 10-11 knots on a single screw triple expansion engine. FORT DUNVEGAN had the distinction of being the first ship in the fleet to fly the Commodore RFA's pennant. She was scrapped in 1968 at Kaohsuing.

(RFA Archive)

RFA FORT BEAUHARNOIS

RFA FORT BEAUHARNOIS in March 1955 still sported the traditional RFA colour scheme of black hull and light grey upperworks. Although completed as a refrigerated VSIS she was also used as a naval stores carrier. Between 1952-56 FORT BEAUHARNOIS freighted stores between Chatham/Gibraltar/Malta, returning via Plymouth. Late in her career she was similarly employed between the UK and the Far East. Note that she had retained her forward gun bandstand from the war years, part of a 1950 ruling which affected all RFAs. This photograph also shows how the uncluttered stern of the Forts could be easily adapted to take a small helicopter platform. Trials on board her sistership FORT DUQUESNE using helicopters for VERTREP were conducted in 1951. FORT BEAUHARNOIS was sold for scrap in 1962.

(MoD/Crown Copyright)

RFA FORT ROSALIE (1945)

RFA FORT ROSALIE's forward holds and ammunition hoists are prominent in this photograph taken towards the end of her time in service. Powered lifts for cargo working were fitted in all three Fort Class armament carriers at the end of the 1950's. A crane, of the type used on the succeeding Ness Class, and possibly fitted for experimental purposes, is visible aft. FORT ROSALIE saw service in the Korean war and was used to return stored ammunition from Australia and South Africa. In 1957 she supported the Christmas Island nuclear bomb tests. She was laid up in Rosyth in 1972 and scrapped the next year in Spain.   (MoD/Crown Copyright)

RFA FORT SANDUSKY

RFA FORT SANDUSKY was acquired while under construction in 1945. She was completed as an NSIS under commercial management and on transferring to the Admiralty in 1949 converted to an ASIS, hence the prominent red band on the funnel. Together with her sister FORT ROSALIE, she differed in appearance with a continuous bridge and boat deck amidships. Note the "A" frame paravane, bow protection gear against moored mines, part of a post-war defensive measure which applied to all but a few auxiliaries. FORT SANDUSKY was involved in the Suez Crisis in 1956 although she spent the bulk of her career in the Far East. She was scrapped in Spain in 1973.

(MoD/Crown Copyright)

RFA SURF PATROL

RFA SURF PATROL, together with her sister SURF PIONEER, were commandeered in 1951 during the Korean War whilst under construction for Poland by the Sunderland firm of Bartram and Sons Ltd. These 11,000 tons deadweight tankers had a service speed of 12.5 knots being powered by a Richardson, Westgarth Doxford four cylinder diesel engine. SURF PATROL was surplus to requirements in the aftermath of the war but spent several years on lucrative charters to various oil companies, still RFA manned. Later she was used for a short while on naval freighting duties before being laid up. SURF PIONEER spent even less time in active service and was placed in reserve by the end of the 1950's. Both ships were sold in 1969. (MoD/Crown Copyright)

RFA SEA FOX

RFA SEA FOX was one of an original order for seven naval aviation store carriers. Only this 700 ton vessel, built by J. Pollock and Sons at Faversham, Kent, flew the RFA ensign. Entering service in January 1952 SEA FOX was employed mainly as an aircraft transport plying between Northern Ireland and the West Coast of Scotland and England and was equipped with twelve ton and six ton cargo handling derricks. Later she was used in the general store ship role. Four of her sisterships performed a similar function but were RN manned. SEAFOX was sold out of service in 1959.

(MoD/Crown Copyright)

RFA EDDYCREEK

RFA EDDYCREEK, a fleet attendant oiler, formed part of an original order for ten ships of which eight were finally constructed between 1951-1954. Rapid post-war advances in RAS practices meant that the 2,000 ton Eddy Class, earmarked as station ships, rapidly became obsolescent. Moreover, for their size, they had a modest 1,650 ton cargo capacity which included 50 tons of lubricating oil carried in special tanks. The gradual withdrawal of forces from East of Suez in the 1960's spelt the end for these ships and EDDYCREEK was sold in 1963 having spent a large proportion of her service based at Hong Kong. (MoD/Crown Copyright)

RFA EDDYFIRTH

The penultimate ship in her class to be completed, RFA EDDYFIRTH also survived considerably longer then her sisterships and was not sold for scrap until 1982. This photograph shows the extensive accommodation spaces which made the Eddy Class comfortable station ships in which to serve. They were constructed on the combined transverse and longitudinal system of framing and driven by enclosed triple expansion steam engines on a single screw. EDDYFIRTH spent a large part of her career in the Mediterranean in support of the Malta Motor Minesweeper flotillas. Later she was employed in UK waters freighting Avcat aviation fuel and lubricating oils.

(RFA Archive)

RFA AMHERST

The profile of armament carrier AMHERST displayed her unmistakable origins as a cargo/passenger ship. Built in 1936 for the Furness Line, she was used on the East Coast American run until declared redundant in 1951. She entered RFA service in 1952, effectively replacing NAV BEDENHAM which had been destroyed in an explosion at Gibraltar the previous year. In poor material condition when acquired, AMHERST needed extensive work on her hull together with replacement boilers. Her deadweight capacity of 2,173 tons was considered adequate for freighting duties; in addition she was capable of carrying twelve passengers. Unsurprisingly, given her previous role, AMHERST proved a popular ship in which to serve. Her relatively short RFA career ended in 1964.   (RFA Archive)

RFA TIDEREACH

The commissioning of the three Tide Class oilers in 1955/6 represented an important new phase for the service. These were the first RFA tankers specifically built to replenish warships at sea. This view of TIDEREACH in ballast in 1962 shows the cohesive design of the Swan Hunter built ship with three replenishment points to port and two on the starboard side, all sited on a single RAS deck. The lattice-style derricks, served by a sophisticated system of self-tensioning winches, were of a new design as were the 6-inch hoses they supported which allowed a higher pumping rate. TIDEREACH was part of the replenishment group supporting the 1961 Kuwait operation. She was scrapped in 1979.

(MoD/Crown Copyright)

RFA TIDESURGE (and GAMBIA)

RFA TIDESURGE refuelling the cruiser GAMBIA during Exercise Dawn Breeze in March 1959. Her single screw double reduction geared turbines provided 15,000 shp to drive the ship at 18 knots. The ship's speed and 15,000 tons cargo capacity were greatly superior to that of the Waves which these Tide Class vessels began to replace in the mid-1950's. As a "4-product tanker" TIDESURGE was equipped to carry Furnace Fuel Oil, Dieso, Avcat and Mogas. Notably, the design of these otherwise advanced auxiliaries lacked any provision for operating helicopters the value of which had yet to be recognised properly in replenishment operations. Previously, TIDESURGE had been named TIDERANGE. The similarity of "-range" and "-race" on distorted radio circuits caused the changes to be made, TIDERACE becoming TIDEFLOW.

(MoD/Crown Copyright)

RFA TIDEFLOW

RFA TIDEFLOW preparing to refuel USS INTREPID in heavy seas in the North Atlantic while en-route for Norfolk, Virginia in December 1967. Understandably, there was concern at the time that the stability required for replenishment serials to be undertaken successfully in high sea states might be compromised by the additional top-weight carried by these tankers in the form of RAS derricks, automatic tensioning winches and sundry conventional winches. Despite proving her worth in that respect, by the mid-seventies TIDEFLOW had been disposed of after barely twenty years service. A fourth ship in the class was built tor the Australian Navy but was loaned to Britain in the period 1955-62 and named, appropriately, RFA TIDE AUSTRAL. (US Navy)

CHUNGKING

Less than two years after the China Navigation Company's cargo and passenger liners CHANGCHOW and CHUNGKING (pictured here) were completed they were declared redundant due to overstocking on the Hong Kong/China/Australia trade route. Acquired by the Admiralty in 1952, CHUNGKING was then employed on mercantile charter work. When this photograph was taken the same year she was still being managed by Buries, Markes Ltd. as evidenced by the firm's distinctive funnel colours. She was converted into a naval stores carrier by Palmers, Hebburn in 1954-5, having been renamed RETAINER in December 1952.   (MoD/Crown Copyright)

RFA RELIANT (1954)

The second RELIANT was built in 1954 as a grain carrier. She traded for two years between the UK and Mexico before being purchased by the Admiralty and converted to her new role at North Shields becoming the RFA's first dedicated Air Stores Issuing Ship capable of replenishing carriers at sea. To this end she was equipped with over 40,000 different patterns of aircraft spares. Originally a five hold, two deck ship, RELIANT had 700 tons of permanent ballast placed on her tank tops and an additional steel deck added. Extra generating power was provided together with state of the art automatic tensioning winches for transfer of stores in unfavourable weather conditions. Affectionately known as "The Yacht", she entered service as RFA SOMERSBY before being renamed in 1958.

(MoD/Crown Copyright)

RFA RIPPLEDYKE (Top)

RFA RIPPLEDYKE, a 975 tons freighting tanker is photographed alongside at the Isle of Grain Refinery in June 1954 while on charter to the Bulk Oil Company. Built for the Ministry of Transport as an "Empire T" she was acquired by the navy in June 1951 in anticipation of the increased demands of the Korean War. In common with the larger Surf Class, RIPPLEDYKE saw little active naval service spending most of her time on charter. She was not RFA manned until 1958 when she was sent to Gibraltar for use as a fuel hulk. At the end of the 1950's the moves to rationalise the RFA fleet in line with perceived future requirements led to the sale of the ship in March 1960.

(RFA Archive)

RFA RESURGENT (Left)

RFA RESURGENT in the process of replenishing ARK ROYAL in the Indian Ocean in May 1966. Both RESURGENT and RETAINER were fitted with helicopter platforms aft reflecting the growing importance of VERTREP during RAS serials. Officially rated as "Fast Fleet Replenishment Ships", the Retainer Class, powered by six-cylinder Scott-Doxford diesels, were capable of 16 knots and were therefore less of an encumbrance than the 11 knot Fort Class for a navy which was rapidly becoming more dependent on sustained operations at sea. RESURGENT was laid up at Rosyth in 1979 and sold to Spanish breakers in March 1981.

(RFA Archive)

RFA BUSTLER

A number of tugs were manned and managed by the RFA in the period after World War II. Unlike other RFAs, their specialist crews did not exchange with other vessels in the fleet. BUSTLER, photographed here, was transferred to the RFA in 1959 having been on charter to Metal Industries (Salvage) Ltd., Faslane between 1947-58. The diesel-engined, 1,100 tons grt. BUSTLER had been built by Henry Robb at Leith and was completed in June 1942 as an ocean going rescue and salvage tug. She had served under the white ensign for the first five years of her career.

(James R. Smith Collection)

RFA APPLELEAF (1955)

The seven strong Leaf Class were acquired in 1959-60 on bareboat charter to serve as freighting tankers and as such progressively replaced a mixed fleet of "Waves", "Dales" and "Surfs". Increasing standardisation within the RFA meant that the Leaf Class, including APPLELEAF here, were all classified as "three product tankers" carrying furnace fuel oil (FFO), Dieso and AVCAT. They were all equipped for astern fuelling, as evident in this photograph, together with the means to receive the abeam refuelling rigs of fleet replenishment ships for inter-tanker transfer. In March 1961 she officially opened the new Henderson Graving Dock at Immingham. The second ship to bear the name in RFA service, APPLELEAF's charter ended in January 1970.   (RFA Archive)

RFA ORANGELEAF (1955)

RFA ORANGELEAF, together with PEARLEAF and PLUMLEAF, differed from the rest of the class in terms of RAS capability, The trio of tankers were progressively fitted with rigs for abeam refuelling; in fact ORANGELEAF had limited capabilities in this respect from the beginning of her charter in 1960. Although of a standard approaching that of the Tide Class in terms of replenishment gantries, ORANGELEAF was not equipped with the modern-style derricks of her fleet tanker contemporaries. She was of a similar gross tonnage to the two "P" Leafs but ORANGELEAF's deadweight of 17,475 tons was smaller. She was used during the 1961 Kuwait Crisis and was returned to her owners in May 1978.

(MoD/Crown Copyright)

RFA PLUMLEAF (1961)

RFA PLUMLEAF was completed in July 1960 and placed on bareboat charter to the Admiralty the following month. The charter was extended in part due to the onset of the Falklands War in 1982. She sailed south on 19 April with REGENT and two frigates. PLUMLEAF's RAS capability, albeit limited, enabled her to function as a "motorway tanker" refuelling warships on passage south and north. At one point she replenished the BRISTOL group, a task which took thirty two hours of which twenty two were spent connected to one or other warship. During the period 19 April to 26 August, PLUMLEAF issued 20,000 tons of fuel, in fifty five separate operations and received in turn 11,000 tons of fuel from STUFT tankers.

(MoD/Crown Copyright)

RFA BROWN RANGER

An interested audience aboard the Royal Yacht looks on as BROWN RANGER's fuel hose is manipulated by HMY BRITANNIA's crew. The two troughs supporting the hose, which in turn are suspended from the auxiliary's single abeam derrick, are clearly visible. What looks like a tarpaulin screen is protecting BRITANNIA's paintwork in the event of a spillage caused by an emergency uncoupling of the hose. This photograph, taken in 1961, shows the limited and dated RAS equipment aboard the ageing auxiliary. BROWN RANGER was the last of her class to be disposed of when she was broken up in 1975. (MoD/Crown Copyright)

RFA BACCHUS (1962)

The third RFA vessel to carry the name was built by Henry Robb at Leith for the BISN and was engined with a Swan-Hunter Sulzer SRD68 turbo-charged five cylinder diesel. She was a direct replacement for FORT CONSTANTINE. BACCHUS was chartered by the Admiralty in 1962 to serve as a solid stores freighter running between Chatham and Singapore via Gibraltar, Malta and Aden. The provision of RAS capability was ruled out as non-cost effective at an early stage. The two ships carried "Chacons", small containers designed for the purpose by Chatham Dockyard, which held four-wheeled trolleys loaded with naval stores. BACCHUS was returned to her owners in 1981.

(M. J. Lennon)

RFA HEBE

The 4,823 tons grt. HEBE entered service in 1962 under the same charter and management terms as her sister BACCHUS. As well as "Chacon" containers, these stores ship could carry 500 tons of water cargo, 210 tons of lubricating oil together with refrigerated stores. On a return trip from Singapore in 1967, HEBE transported three aircraft and two Naval Store tenders on her upper deck in addition to the cargo in her holds. The containerisation system pioneered by this pair, together with the use of fork-lift trucks and portable rollers for cargo handling, were developed more extensively in the succeeding Ness, Resource and Fort Classes of stores ships.

(K. Johnson)

RFA DISCOVERY

Confusingly, the previous RFA named DISCOVERY was known as RFA DIS-COVERY II in deference to Captain Scott's famous ship of the same name which was still in service. This 2,667 tons grt. Royal Research vessel, built by Hall Russell in 1962, was powered by three six-cylinder Ruston Hornsby diesel electric engines which gave her a range of 15,000 miles at 10 knots. DISCOVERY was ice-strengthened and equipped with a bow-thruster. There were laboratory spaces and workshops for up to twenty scientists together with a raft containing acoustic equipment at the bottom of a vertical trunkwell which could be raised and lowered for the purpose of underwater research. The ship was last manned with a RFA crew in 1969.

(MoD/Crown Copyright)

RFA TIDEPOOL

Both the Hebburn built Improved Tide Class Fleet Tankers entered service in 1963. TIDEPOOL, photographed here, replaced WAVE SOVEREIGN in the RFA Fleet. There was opposition to the inclusion of helicopter facilities at the design stage; their value in auxiliaries had yet to be fully realised. The ship's five abeam replenishment points and astern refuelling equipment are visible here. These provided the tankers with an overall pumping capacity of 2,400 tons per hour. TIDEPOOL acted as a support ship during the 1975-76 Cod War. The ship was on passage to transfer to the Chilean Navy in 1982 when she was recalled at the start of the Falklands War. Tthe ship subsequently played a prominent part in the conflict before being restored to her new owners who renamed her ALMIRANTE JORGE MoNTT.

(MoD/Crown Copyright)

RFA TIDESPRING

RFA TIDESPRING, the replacement for WAVE MASTER, about to enter harbour attended by the Portsmouth based TUTTs ADEPT and POWERFUL. The Improved Tides had a cargo capacity of 14,200 tons, typically comprising FFO, Avcat, Mogas, drinking water and dry goods. They were designed for a service speed of 17 knots in deep load conditions on their double reduction geared turbines; a sacrifice of two knots was made on the original specification in order to avoid delays in construction. Specially strengthened hulls for combating Arctic ice together with the ability to heat and maintain FFO at 90°F indicate the anticipated areas of operation at the height of the Cold War. TIDESPRING's 28 years in service ended in 1991 by which time she had steamed 1,270,388 nautical miles.

(W. Sartori)

RFA OLWEN

The 1961 Kuwait Crisis underlined the need for "front-line support ships" capable of sustaining fleet speed in support of naval task groups. From an original requirement for six "19½ knot tankers" emerged the three Ol Class, including OLWEN photographed here. The design was based on the successful "Improved Tide" but these larger ships were fitted with four goalpost gantries and no fewer than seven abeam and two astern refuelling rigs. OLWEN, originally built as OLYNTHUS but renamed in August 1967, spent eleven weeks on station during the last Cod War (1975-76) and had the distinction of being the first RFA to support the Armilla Patrol in 1980. By the end of 1999 she was laid up at Portsmouth and commenced her final voyage to Turkish breakers in February 2001.

(MoD/Crown Copyright)

RFA OLMEDA

The Swan Hunter built OLMEDA is seen here in the Channel early in her career. The intricate arrangement of self-tensioning winches, derricks and hoses is evident in this photograph together with the large port side hangar capable of accommodating up to three helicopters. In common with the Tide Class, the three Ol's were "four product ships" with some additional capacity for the carriage of water, dry stores and drummed lubricating oils. They were engined with Parmetrada double reduction geared turbines rated at 26,500 shp which provided a maximum speed of 21 knots. The three ships of the class first commissioned 1965-66. OLMEDA was the first of the trio to be disposed of in 1994.   (MoD/Crown Copyright)

RFA TARBATNESS

TARBATNESS is seen here preparing to transfer stores to NUBIAN in the South China Sea in March 1970. All three of the diesel engined Ness Class were built by Swan Hunter and entered service in 1966/67. TARBATNESS, and her sister STROMNESS, were designated naval and victualling stores ships. Their cargo included about 40,000 different items of naval stores and 15,000 man months of victualling stores including 37,000 cubic feet of beer! Replacing the outmoded Fort Class, these Admiralty designed ships were intended for world-wide deployment and as such were fully air-conditioned with modern facilities for their crews. Declared surplus to requirements and in reserve at Gibraltar TARBATNESS was first leased and then purchased (in 1982) by the U.S. Military Sealift Command for further service.

(RFA Archive)

RFA STROMNESS

This photograph affords an excellent view of STROMNESS's helicopter deck and the cargo lift used during VERTREP serials. At the design stage, consideration was given to the fitting of a helicopter hangar but this idea was dismissed due to budgetary constraints. At the start of the Falklands War on 2 April 1982 STROMNESS was de-stored at Portsmouth and awaiting disposal. Five days later, fully stored and with 350 members of 45 Commando embarked, she sailed south. After being the first RFA to enter Falkland Sound, STROMNESS then endured some of the worst of the bombing in San Carlos Water. Eventually she returned to Portsmouth having issued 2912 pallets and landed nearly 750 troops. Like her sisters, STROMNESS was then sold to the U.S. Military Sealift Command.

(MoD/Crown Copyright)

RFA LYNESS

Unlike her two sisters, LYNESS was completed as an Air Stores Support Ship. It was the intention to build a fourth 19.5- knot "stretched" version of the class as a dedicated Air Stores ship but this plan did not materialise. The cohesive design of these purpose-built, under-way replenishment RFAs is evident in this photograph. The cargo was kept in four temperature and humidity controlled holds. Movement of stores by fork-lift trucks and powered roller transporters was facilitated by the 320 foot clearway deck which provided access through 12 foot wide, hydraulically operated watertight doors to one of five jackstay transfer points. LYNESS replaced FORT DUQUESNE in the fleet.

(K. Johnson)

RFA ENGADINE

Royal Navy manpower shortages in the mid-1960's resulted in the helicopter support ship RFA ENGADINE commissioning as a RFA, albeit with a permanent RN detachment. Accepted into service in January 1967, ENGADINE's specialist roles were defined as deep water anti-submarine and anti-ship operational flying training, deck landing practice and flight team training. Intensive 2-3 week training schedules meant that ENGADINE was at sea for between 60-70% of the time. This photograph shows the ship towards the end of her career with a lengthened flight deck which enabled her to operate two Sea Kings simultaneously. (MoD/Crown Copyright)

RFA REGENT

Commissioned in 1967, REGENT and RESOURCE were the first purpose-built RFA Fleet Replenishment ships. Although their cargo included a range of stores they were principally armament carriers and to this end the size of present and future weapons were determining factors in their design. These ships had stowage for up to 80 Sea Slug missiles; an extra heavy-duty jackstay for handling these bulky weapons was sited on the port side aft. Flat topped electrical lifts serving all cargo spaces, the latest mechanical handling devices and a clear passage along the upper deck were seen as essential requirements if these ships were to function effectively for 30 days in the operational area. REGENT was disposed of in 1992.

(Stuart Talton)

RFA RESOURCE

The 23,000 ton RESOURCE was built by Scotts at Greenock. She had a long career, taking part in naval operations at Aden, Cyprus, Rhodesia, the Falklands and the Gulf. In 1982 she supported the Battle Group throughout the war, issuing nearly 4,000 pallets of stores to warships and land forces via helicopter. One of the first auxiliaries to anchor in San Carlos Water, RESOURCE was present during some of the fiercest bombing raids. In 1992 she commenced a five year stint as a "floating warehouse" in Croatia in support of British forces in the former Yugoslavia. Plans to maintain her in reserve or to sell her for future service did not materialise and the ship departed for the scrapyard in 1997.   (MoD/Crown Copyright)

ARK MULTI-RAS
Part of the 1960's East of Suez policy was the formation of Underway Replenishment Groups consisting of fast, purpose-built auxiliaries capable of supporting carrier task force operations. Here is the concept in action with TIDESURGE using two of her port rigs to RAS(L) with ARK ROYAL. The stores chutes in position on ARK's forward lift opening suggests that a VERTREP serial with the Air Stores Support ship LYNESS (nearest the camera) is imminent or has just completed. The frigate manoeuvring on the far side of the group is ESKIMO.

(MoD/Crown Copyright)

RFA DEWDALE (1965)

The withdrawal of British Forces from Aden in 1967 meant that large capacity freighting tankers were required to ensure the supply of fuel for the Navy east of Suez. To fill this gap three modern, commercial tankers were acquired on bareboat charter. All three of the new Dale Class were named after the wartime LSGs and underwent limited modification. DEWDALE II (ex-EDENFIELD) is photographed here in May 1970 in the Indian Ocean. She has just refuelled FEARLESS; her hose can be seen trailing astern on the port side aft. She had a deadweight of 60,600 tons on 40 feet draught and was fitted with a 17,000hp nine-cylinder Burmeister and Wain diesel engine. DEWDALE's period of service was the longest of the three Mobile Reserve tankers ending in September 1977 when she was returned to her owners.

(J. Asquith)

89

RFA ENNERDALE (1963)

The smallest of the three Mobile Reserve tankers, the 47,470 ton ENNERDALE (ex-NAESS SCOTSMAN) is photographed in September 1969 in contemporary RFA colour scheme. In June 1969 the ship had been awarded the Wilkinson Sword of Peace and in April the following year was on Indian Ocean standby during the Apollo 13 splashdown. However, on 1 June 1970 the ship struck a submerged reef off the Seychelles and sank, fortunately with no loss of life. The subsequent oil spillage, which temporarily threatened the islands, was cleared but salvaging ENNERDALE proved impossible. The wreck was finally broken up with explosives, including A/S mortars and torpedo warheads, which were brought to the scene by a helicopter operated from RFA STROMNESS.

(MoD/Crown Copyright)

RFA DERWENTDALE (1965)

RFA DERWENTDALE (ex-HALCYON BREEZE) had a deadweight of 73,375 tons making her the largest of the three Dale Class tankers and the largest ship to serve in the RFA. Built by Hitachi Zosen of Innoshima, Japan when fully loaded the ship displaced 88,555 tons. The withdrawal of naval forces from the Gulf and the Far East in the autumn of 1971 contributed to the reduction in need for vessels of this capacity. DERWENTDALE was returned to her owners in June 1974.

(MoD/Crown Copyright)

DERWENTDALE

RFA BLACK ROVER

The Swan Hunter built Rover Class of small fleet tankers entered service in the period 1969-74 replacing the Ranger Class. BLACK ROVER, photographed soon after commissioning for the first time in 1974, has often been assigned to FOST during her career. The distinctive appearance of these ships is apparent here with the main superstructure and bridge sited two thirds of the way to the stern to accommodate a large helicopter platform which extends aft from the boat deck. As "four product" tankers, each vessel has a cargo capacity of 6,600 tons of fuel. There is additional capacity for fresh water, dry cargo and refrigerated stores which can be delivered to the flight deck via a two ton capacity lift. (MoD/Crown Copyright)

RFA BLUE ROVER

The first three in the Rover Class, GREEN, GREY and BLUE (pictured here) were initially fitted with two Ruston AO 16 cylinder diesel engines - an installation partly introduced to enable maintenance work to be undertaken with the ships underway. The RFA's first venture into propulsion by medium speed, high-powered diesel machinery proved unsuccessful and the trio were expensively re-engined in the period 1973-74. BLUE ROVER was the only one of her class to sail south during the Falklands War initially acting as South Georgia station tanker. Later she replenished ships in the anchorages at San Carlos and Port William and refuelled no fewer than 150 helicopters. BLUE ROVER was sold to Portugal in 1993 and re-named NRP BERRIO.

(MoD/Crown Copyright)

BLUE ROVER

A270

RFA GOLD ROVER

RFA GOLD ROVER abeam refuelling with a Sir Lancelot Class LSL in the Portland Exercise Area while her astern refuelling hose is extended ready for use on the ship's port side. Rover Class tankers are fitted with a single "goalpost" gantry and two large derrick rigs, one on each side. The ship routinely supports the Royal Navy's presence in the Caribbean region and has played a significant part over the years in disaster relief and drug smuggling countermeasures. In September 1977 GOLD ROVER successfully undertook an experimental "pump-over" in the Channel with an otherwise unmodified BP tanker BRITISH TAMAR. This was timely in view of events less than five years later although GREY ROVER had conducted initial RAS trials with BRITISH ESK in July 1976.

(MoD/Crown Copyright)

RFA GREY ROVER

A busy scene at Portland in 1986, with GREY ROVER berthed at the Outer Coaling Pier, GREEN ROVER and GOLD ROVER astern and OLNA in the distance at "G" Anchorage. During the Falklands War, GREY ROVER acted as "resident work-up tanker" for FOST conducting replenishment trials and training with chartered merchant ships including QE2 and ATLANTIC CONVEYOR. Too small to work alone with a large task force, the Rovers have provided ideal support for individual warships or small groups on deployment. To this end GREY ROVER has often been assigned to accompany the RN's South Atlantic patrol. According to latest forecasts the Rover Class are due to be phased out by 2007 when the remaining ships will be over 30 years old. (MoD/Crown Copyright)

RFA SIR BEDIVERE (Army Dept.)

The MoD, through the Army Department, employed BISN as agents to manage and crew the six Sir Lancelot Class Landing Ship Logistic (LSL) in the period from completion to their transfer to the RFA. Hence SIR BEDIVERE, seen here on station in Far Eastern waters, is in traditional trooping colours of white hull and upperworks with a blue band around the hull. The change in management was introduced for quite complex financial as well as operational reasons, negotiations were protracted and transfer did not take place until the period January to March 1970. These LSLs were built to replace an ageing group of war-construction landing ships which included EMPIRE GULL which was retained and also transferred to RFA management.

(MoD/Crown Copyright)

RFA SIR GERAINT

RFA SIR GERAINT was the third in her class to commission in March 1968. The 5,674 tonnes ship, part landing craft, part Ro-Ro ferry, is desgned to land troops, vehicles, tanks and other heavy equipment either in port or directly to a beach head. Selfpropelled mexe-flotes, of the type seen here strapped to SIR GERAINT's starboard side, work from the vessel's stern ramp. These floating platforms provide the LSLs with useful flexibility in amphibious operations. SIR GERAINT will be replaced by one of the Alternative Landing Ship Logistic (ALSL) being built from 2001.

(MoD/Crown Copyright)

RFA SIR LANCELOT

As the prototype, the Fairfield built SIR LANCELOT differed in detail from the rest of the class. She is seen here leaving Portsmouth following the Falklands Campaign. Two days after arriving in Falkland Sound, SIR LANCELOT was hit twice by 1,000lb bombs which fortunately failed to explode but put her out of action for three weeks. Note the 40mm gun mounted forward, part of a consignment of eight brought south by MV ELK to provide three of the LSLs with limited self defence. Following RFA service, and before sale to the Singapore Navy, she was used as a cross-Channel ferry and as a floating casino off South Africa. (RFA Archive)

RFA EMPIRE GULL

RFA EMPIRE GULL leaving Marchwood for the last time in 1978 with the signal hoist "Going for a Song". She was laid down in Canada in 1944 as LST 3523 and in 1970 became the only Landing Ship Tank ever to be operated by the RFA. The ship spent her first decade in reserve but was renamed HMS TROUNCER in 1947. Following Suez, she was converted for service as a military transport under civilian contract, at which point she became EMPIRE GULL. As a RFA she was registered for the carriage of non-perishable cargoes and used mainly on the Marchwood/Antwerp run. Note the change in pennant number from her LST days and the retention of the black hull from her time under contract to BISN.

(James R. Smith Collection)

RFA CHERRYLEAF (1963)

The third CHERRYLEAF is photographed at anchor in April 1973 shortly after her acquisition by the fleet. She replaced CHERRYLEAF II whose short period on charter ended in 1966. Although the original seven of this Leaf Class differed quite markedly in appearance they were similarly engined with six-cylinder Doxford diesels except for this tanker which had a seven-cylinder MAN diesel. The primary function of the freighting tanker, as defined in the "60/88 Plan", was to bring bulk supplies from Main bases and Support Areas in order to replenish Front Line and Forward Base Support Ships. CHERRYLEAF's hose for astern refuelling is clearly seen on her port side together with the forward mast which could be rigged for jackstay transfer. CHERRYLEAF's charter ended in 1980.

(MoD/Crown Copyright)

RFAs FORT GRANGE & FORT AUSTIN

The design of FORT GRANGE and FORT AUSTIN was based on the successful and popular Ness Class. The Scott-Lithgow built ships entered service in 1978 and 1979 respectively.. In this picture FORT GRANGE and FORT AUSTIN exchange patrol in the South Atlantic in December 1982. Their capability to operate four Sea King helicopters was used in the months following the Falklands War when one or other auxiliary provided the forward operating base for ASW aircraft in the vicinity of the islands. The need for heightened security explains the absence of pennant numbers and deck code markings on the two ships; note that FORT AUSTIN's name has also been painted over. Defensive armament in the form of single 20mm AA gun mountings are sited on the twin SCOT platforms atop the super-structure on both ships.

(MoD/Crown Copyright)

RFA FORT AUSTIN

RFA FORT AUSTIN replenishing the Type 42 destroyer BIRMINGHAM in the early 1980's. A Sea King HAS2, with underslung load, hovers between the two vessels. At the same time, a jackstay ammunition transfer is taking place using FORT AUSTIN's forward port replenishment station. The ship has three sliding stay, constant-tension transfer rigs on each side which are accessed from her four holds. FORT AUSTIN won a Falklands Battle Honour, served during the Gulf War and in the Adriatic and in 2000 accompanied the Amphibious Ready Group in operations off the coast of Sierra Leone. (MoD/Crown Copyright)

RFA FORT ROSALIE (1978)

RFA FORT GRANGE was renamed FORT ROSALIE in 2000 to avoid confusion with FORT GEORGE. The ships displace 22,749 tons fl. and carry up to 3,500 tons of ammunition and victualling stores. The RFA crew is supplemented by 30 civilians from the Royal Navy Supply and Transport Service, together with up to 45 RN personnel if a full complement of aircraft is embarked. FORT ROSALIE came to prominence in 2000-2001 when she provided alongside engineering support, stores and accommodation during the nuclear submarine TIRELESS's lengthy and controversial sojourn at Gibraltar.

(D. Ferro)

RFA RESOURCE/REGENT & MV SCOTTISH EAGLE

The Fleet Replenishment ships RESOURCE (nearest the camera) and REGENT amidst the splendour of South Georgia shortly after the end of the Falklands Campaign. In the background is the STUFT SCOTTISH EAGLE acting in the capacity of station "fuel depot". The tug, just visible on the port side of the King Line tanker, is probably the SALVAGEMAN. Prominent in this photograph are the replenishment ships' helicopter decks. At sixty feet above the waterline, they were higher than those of contemporary aircraft carriers.

(MoD/Crown Copyright)

RFA SIR TRISTRAM

RFA SIR TRISTRAM lying in Port Stanley Harbour in September 1982. Her distorted and blackened superstructure bears witness to the horrific fires which swept through the LSL following the fateful raid at Fitzroy Cove three months previously. Initially abandoned, SIR TRISTRAM was sea-lifted home by the Heavy Transport vessel DAN LIFTER. The ship was subsequently extensively refitted and updated. Ten metres were added to her length and her new superstructure was constructed of steel rather than aluminium. Returning to service in 1985 she has since demonstrated the innate versatility of the class coordinating disaster work off Central America in the wake of Hurricane Mitch and operating in the MCMV Command and Support Ship role, providing engineering support in the process.

(RFA Archive)

OLWEN, FEARLESS & INVINCIBLE

Three of the Royal Navy's largest ships of the time are seen in close company. OLWEN (minus her pennant number A122) is refuelling the aircraft carrier INVINCIBLE using her port forward rig while FEARLESS, with a line attached to the tanker's bows, is stationed on the starboard side. Judging by the angle of OLWEN's starboard aft derrick, the assault ship is also about to take on fuel.

(MoD / Crown Copyright)

RFA BAYLEAF (1982)

The 37,747 tonnes Leaf Class Support Tanker BAYLEAF running light in this 1986 photograph. In 1975 Cammell Laird assumed ownership of an order for four STAT 32 product tankers three of which were under construction when their client ran into financial difficulties. Two, APPLELEAF (now HMAS WESTRALIA) and ORANGELEAF, were subsequently chartered by MoD(N) while a third, BRAMBLELEAF, was purchased outright. The fourth ship in thé original order was also completed, emerging as RFA BAYLEAF. Bareboat chartered in March 1982, she sailed the next month for Portland, Ascension Island and the Falklands. Although principally assigned to freighting tasks, BAYLEAF also supported the Carrier Task Group. During the war the tanker handled 160,000 cubic metres of fuel and 100 helicopter transfers.

(MoD/Crown Copyright)

RFA ORANGELEAF (1982)

RFA ORANGELEAF keeping close company with the Type 22 frigate BEAVER during Group Uniform's Gulf deployment in early 1990. Note the radar signature reducing matting lining the ship's superstructure and the considerable amount of stores on the main deck. This STAT 32 tanker (as BALDER LONDON) was requisitioned for war service in 1982 and employed on freighting duties as part of the Atlantic logistics chain with RFA communications and RAS teams aboard. She was bareboat chartered and renamed ORANGELEAF in 1985, her conversion to RFA being undertaken at Falmouth and on the Tyne. The ship has been regularly used as Arabian Gulf Ready Tanker. Over the past decade crew rotations have enabled these support tankers to undertake prolonged out of area deployments some lasting two years.

(MoD/Crown Copyright)

RFA SIR CARADOC

RFA SIR CARADOC (ex MV GREY MASTER) with stern ramp lowered and a full complement of vehicles on her upper deck during exercises in Northern Waters in January 1986. Both SIR CARADOC and SIR LAMORAK were acquired on bareboat charter in January 1983 following the loss of SIR GALAHAD and the extensive damage to SIR TRISTRAM during the Falklands War. The 25-ton crane on the former Ro-Ro ferry's port side was removed from SIR TRISTRAM while the LSL was under repair on the Tyne Powered by twin screws, the ship has a deadweight tonnage of 3,350 tonnes and a range of 10,000 nautical miles.SIR CARADOC was returned to her owners in June 1988 after 5 years service in the RFA. (MoD/Crown Copyright)

RFA SIR LAMORAK

SIR LAMORAK, formerly MV LAKESPAN ONTARIO, is photographed off Portland in the spring of 1983 during her work-up with RFA SIR CARADOC. SIR LAMORAK had a DWT of 2,566 tonnes, a maximum speed of 17 knots and a range of 12,000 nautical miles. Unequipped for the carriage of troops and lacking helicopter landing facilities, the principal role of the two replacements LSLs was confined to the movement of vehicles and stores. SIR LAMORAK deployed to the South Atlantic but reputedly only reached Ascension when, due to excessive rolling, the voyage was terminated. Her brief RFA service ended in January 1986.   (MoD/Crown Copyright)

RFA DILIGENCE (with REGENT)

RFA DILIGENCE "collecting" the frigate PENELOPE from alongside REGENT in San Carlos Water in September 1985. The STUFT tug IRISHMAN is also in view. Purchased from Stena UK in October 1983, DILIGENCE underwent a two month £28 million conversion at Clyde Dock Engineering. Features added included a large workshop for hull and machinery repairs, extra accommodation space, extensive craneage facilities, the provision of overside services for ships alongside, naval victualling and armament stores and a naval communications suite. Her existing diving facilities were supplemented with a decompression chamber. DILIGENCE provides mainte-nance for ships and submarines operating away from their home ports. Additionally, she is the RN's primary battle repair unit tasked to react at short notice worldwide. (MoD/Crown Copyright)

RFA DILIGENCE

The commissioning of DILIGENCE in 1984 marked the return to RFA service of the specialised fleet repair role last undertaken by RFA RELIANCE during WW1. The ship is seen here manoeuvring astern of Hunt Class MCMVs and the survey vessel HERALD. Although DILIGENCE has undertaken lengthy spells of duty in the South Atlantic supporting successive guardships and SSNs on annual deployment she has also performed, as here, the "mothership" role in the Persian Gulf in addition to task group deployments, notably Ocean Wave '97 and NTG 2000. DILIGENCE's capacious well-deck is clearly visible together with her bridge roof flight deck which is capable of landing Chinook size helicopters.

(MoD / Crown Copyright)

RFA RELIANT (1983)

RFA RELIANT (ex-MV ASTRONOMER) photographed in the Falklands in early 1986, was chartered by MoD(N) in 1983 and completed a nine month £25 million conversion to an Aviation Support Ship at Cammell Laird. This acquisition was driven by the need for an ASW helicopter support platform in the Falklands together with the RN's desire to evaluate the U.S. Arapaho system which comprised, in this case, a pre-fabricated flight deck and hangar on RELIANT's main deck. The experiment proved a short-lived and costly failure, despite the ship's involvement in a successful troop and civilian evacuation from Lebanon in 1984. The Arapaho system could not accommodate AEW helicopters and 70 containers were needed to support just five aircraft. RELIANT decommissioned in May 1986.

(RFA Archive)

RFA GREY ROVER/LUTJENS/O'BANNON

An RAF Bucaneer makes a low pass over RFA GREY ROVER as she commences a RAS(L) with the destroyers FGS LUTJENS and USS O'BANNON during NATO Sea Days off Plymouth in July 1984. (Mike Critchley)

RFA OAKLEAF (1985)

The Swedish built RFA OAKLEAF (ex-OKTANIA) at 49,648 tonnes full load is currently the largest vessel in the RFA fleet. She differs considerably from the four STAT 32 tankers in size and appearance, enough to be in a class of her own. Powered by a four-cylinder Burmeister and Wain long stroke oil engine driving a single controllable pitch propeller, OAKLEAF has a service speed of 14 knots. Acquired on a twelve year bareboat charter (since extended) in March 1985 to replace PLUMLEAF, OAKLEAF underwent a £5 million six month conversion at Falmouth in 1986. She emerged with increased accommodation, upgraded communication and navigation equipment plus a raised working deck with two replenishment rigs.   (MoD / Crown Copyright)

RFA SIR GALAHAD (1988)

The loss of the LSL SIR GALAHAD at Fitzroy Creek in June 1982 led to the construction of a replacement with the same name which entered service in 1988. The Swan Hunter built SIR GALAHAD, although similar in profile to her predecessor, features a number of design improvements. The higher propulsive efficiency of her propellers has resulted in an increase in speed while the ship's endurance is now 13,000 nm at 15 knots, 60% greater than the previous ship. Visor type bow doors have replaced the side hinge variety thus improving rough water performance. Other changes have included enhanced accommodation, better internal sub-division and the use of steel rather than aluminium in the superstructure.

(MoD / Crown Copyright)

RFA ARGUS

The Ro-Ro container/vehicle cargo vessel MV CONTENDER BEZANT was purchased by MoD(N) for £13 million in March 1984 and accepted into service as RFA ARGUS in 1988 following a protracted conversion at Harland and Wolff. She replaced the smaller and less capable RFA ENGADINE as Aviation Training Ship. Her large flight deck, encompassing over two thirds of her total length and including five landing spots, enables the 28,000 tonnes ARGUS to operate any of the RN's helicopters. The flexibility offered by this large platform has been fully exploited, as here in the logistic ship role. During her 2001 refit ARGUS was fitted out as a Primary Casualty Receiving Ship, a decade after fulfilling the same task on a temporary basis during Desert Storm.   (MoD/Crown Copyright)

RFAs DILIGENCE and TIDESPRING

RFA TIDESPRING undertaking a RAS(L) with DILIGENCE in the Persian Gulf in August 1988. This period of high tension in the region, following the mining of the Straits of Hormuz, is reflected in the precautions taken against surprise attack with the radar signature reducing material on both ships. DILIGENCE is powered by a diesel-electric plant feeding four 1500 HP electric motors geared to a variable pitch propeller and two 1500 HP variable pitch thrusters. Two further bow thrusters give the ship tremendous manoeuvrability as demonstrated here. A Kongsberg Dynamic Positioning System, linked to propellers and thrusters, enables DILIGENCE to hold station in heavy wind and sea states.

(MoD/Crown Copyright)

RFA FORT GEORGE (This page)

This aerial view of FORT GEORGE affords a good view of her four abeam NEI-Clarke Chapman designed dual purpose RAS stations. A Hudson Reel stern refuelling rig provides a fifth RAS(L) point. The large block between the gantries contains the replenishment control centre with the currently redundant VLS Seawolf silos on the roof. FORT GEORGE and her sistership displace over 31,000 tonnes and their cargo capacity of fuel, stores and ammunition includes 12,505 m³ of liquids and 6,234 m³ of solids. Accommodation and maintenance facilities for up to five Sea King/Merlin helicopters provide the AORs with an aviation capability second only to that of the RN's carriers.

(MoD / Crown Copyright)

RFA FORT VICTORIA (Left)

The Auxiliary Replenishment Oiler (AOR) FORT VICTORIA leaving Portsmouth Naval Base. Eight of these vessels were planned but only two built. The original Cold War inspired concept envisaged each AOR supporting a permanent task force of three "austere" Type 23 frigates in the GIUK Gap. Priorities have changed but the RFA has retained two highly capable vessels equipped with "stealth" features, a sophisticated communications and countermeasures fit and a self-defence armament which includes the Phalanx CIWS. Under a full payload the ship's cargo is likely to exceed the value of the vessel herself. FORT VICTORIA's construction was initially grossly under budgeted resulting in costly delays for fault rectification. These have continued to affect the ship's operational readiness; most recently a lengthy docking period interrupted her participation in NTG2000.

(MoD/Crown Copyright)

RFA SIR BEDIVERE (SLEP)

RFA SIR BEDIVERE is seen here in the Main Basin of the Babcock Rosyth Dockyard on the 4 August 1995 temporarily undocked during her three year SLEP (Ship Life Extension Programme). Alterations to the ship's profile are becoming apparent: twelve metres have been added to her length, her flight deck has been lowered and the accommodation block shifted forward ten metres. Principally, these modifications provide extra space for crew accommodation and embarked troops. "Stealth" features have been added to the re-constructed superstructure. SIR BEDIVERE was also re-engined during the SLEP and given a new propulsion system. The vessel visible in the background is the war vintage ex-HMS STALKER (LST 3515). (Babcock Engineering Services)

RFA SIR BEDIVERE (post-SLEP)

The LSL SIR BEDIVERE photographed at sea post-SLEP. The modifications, which added twelve metres to the length of the ship, included extensive replacement of steel in the hull itself pushing her displacement up to 6,700 tonnes from her original 5,770 tonnes. A new control and surveillance system was installed, linked to an electronic management suite on the bridge. SIR BEDIVERE is also equipped to operate Merlin helicopters from her flight deck and Chinooks from the vehicle deck. However this lengthy refurbishment programme which cost nearly £69 million was considered non cost-effective and has not been extended to sisterships SIR PERCIVALE and SIR GERAINT as originally intended.

(MoD/Crown Copyright)

RFA SEA CRUSADER

The formation of the tri-services Joint Rapid Reaction Force (JRRF), resulted in the bareboat charter of the 23,986 tonnes grt. SEA CRUSADER in late 1996. The JRRF assigned RFAs are required to be on seven days notice to move equipment and troops to a range of ports worldwide. Therefore, at other times, SEA CRUSADER is tasked with routine freighting duties and exercise support, working out of Marchwood. This ship, seen here about to enter Portsmouth Harbour in February 1997, and SEA CENTURION are perceived as interim acquisitions pending the delivery of the first Ro-Ros built under a Private Finance Initiative (PFI) Contract. This probably explains the absence of RFA livery and the fact that SEA CRUSADER's pennant number (A96) is not displayed.

(MoD/Crown Copyright)

RFA SEA CENTURION

The second of the RFA manned JRRF vessels, SEA CENTURION, was acquired by MoD(N) on an eighteen month bareboat charter in October 1998. Her Italian builder ran into financial difficulties which resulted in the non-delivery of a second vessel in this Stena 4-Runner Class which had also been destined for RFA service. SEA CENTURION's three vehicle decks, comprising 2,715 LIMS (linear [lane] metres), are arranged for the rapid loading and discharge of well over 400 vehicles. Her stern ramp is capable of taking heavy armour such as Challenger tanks. SEA CENTURION was used during Operation Agricola, ferrying military equipment destined for the British Army in Kosovo. Her charter period has been extended to July 2002. (Maritime Photographic)

RFA WAVE KNIGHT (2002)

RFA WAVE KNIGHT setting out on her maiden voyage from Barrow where she had been built by BAE Systems. Although comparable in size to the Ol Class they replace, the two Wave Class double-hulled Fleet Replenishment tankers bear more resemblance to the Rovers with their single, large RAS deck forward and bridge superstructure and flight deck set about two thirds of the way to the stern. WAVE KNIGHT's Clarke Chapman designed rigs will deliver the ship's 16,000 m³ of liquids including 3,000 m³ of aviation fuel. Diesel electric powered through a single shaft, WAVE KNIGHT has a service speed of 18 knots and a range of 10,000 nm at 15 knots.

(BAE Systems)

RFA WAVE RULER

Unlike her sistership whose hull and upperworks were constructed in sections in shipyards around the country, WAVE RULER, photographed here shortly atter her launch on the 9 February 2001, was built almost entirely at BAE Systems in Govan. The Clyde yard received the job in preference to Barrow amidst concerns that the latter would be unable to deliver on time due to heavy work load. WAVE RULER will provide RAS(L) and VERTREP tor general purpose task groups and will be capable of supporting and operating Merlin helicopters in conditions up to sea state 6. Her defensive armament will include two 30mm cannon and she will be able to receive two Raytheon Mk. 15 Phalanx CIWS.

(MoD/Crown Copyright)

INDEX